Books in the Linkers series

Homes discovered through Art & Technology
Homes discovered through Geography
Homes discovered through History
Homes discovered through Science

Myself discovered through Art & Technology
Myself discovered through Geography
Myself discovered through History
Myself discovered through Science

Toys discovered through Art & Technology
Toys discovered through Geography
Toys discovered through History
Toys discovered through Science

Water discovered through Art & Technology
Water discovered through Geography
Water discovered through History
Water discovered through Science

First published 1996 A&C Black (Publishers) Limited
35 Bedford Row, London WC1R 4JH

ISBN 0-7136-4351-X
A CIP catalogue record for this book is available from the British Library.

Copyright © 1996 BryantMole Books

Some of the people featured in this book are models.
Commissioned photographs by Zul Mukhida
Design by Jean Wheeler

Consultant: Hazel Grice

Acknowledgements

Chapel Studios; 11 (right), Science Photo Library; 20 (left), 23 (left), Topham Picture Library; 8 (left), WPL; 2 (right), 23 (right), Zefa; 2 (left), 6 (left), 13 (both), 15 (both), 16, 20 (right).

All rights reserved. No part of this publication may be reproduced in any form or by any means – graphic, electronic or mechanical, including photocopying, recording, taping or information storage and retrieval systems – without the prior permission in writing of the publishers.

Printed and bound in Italy by L.E.G.O.

Myself

discovered through
Science

Karen Bryant-Mole

Contents

My body 2
Seeing 4
Hearing 6
Touching 8
Tasting and
   smelling 10
Babies 12
Growing 14
I'm alive 16
Keeping healthy 18
Feeling ill 20
I'm me! 22
Glossary 24
Index 24

A & C Black • London

My body

Although human beings look very different to one another, there are some features that we share.

Bodies
Each of these children has a head, arms, legs and a main body part that is sometimes called a trunk.

Legs
In the middle of each leg there is a joint, called a knee.
This joint allows your leg to bend.
Your feet are at the bottom of your legs.
Each foot has five toes.
Legs and feet help you to walk and jump and climb and run.

Arms

There is a joint in the middle of each arm, too. It is called an elbow.
Your hands are on the end of your arms.
Each hand has five fingers.
What can you do with your hands?

Seeing

You have five senses that help you to know what is going on around you. Seeing is one of your senses.

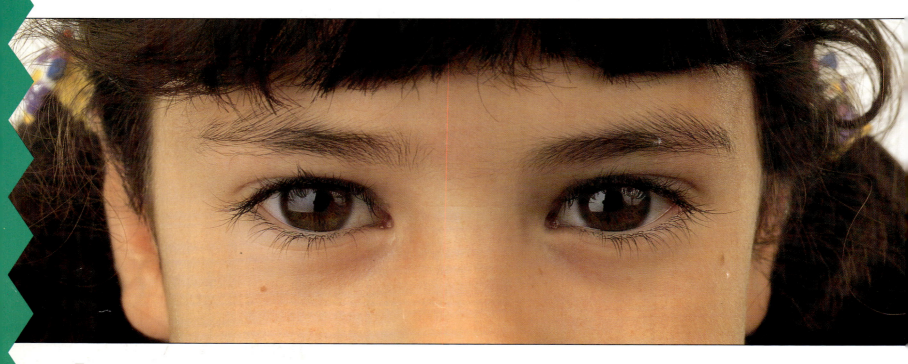

Eyes
You use your eyes to see.
Rays of light go into your eyes and make a picture.
A nerve sends this picture to your brain.

Glasses
Sometimes, people's eyes do not work as well as they should and so they wear glasses.
The glass in glasses helps to improve the picture that is made in the eye.

Information
When you look at an object you see its colour, its shape and its size.
You also see whether it is close to you or far away.

Hearing

Hearing is the sense that helps you recognise sounds.

Ears
Sounds go into your ears and make tiny bones inside your ears wobble. These wobbling bones make ripples in a liquid in your ear.
Nerves in the liquid send messages to your brain, which your brain understands as sound.

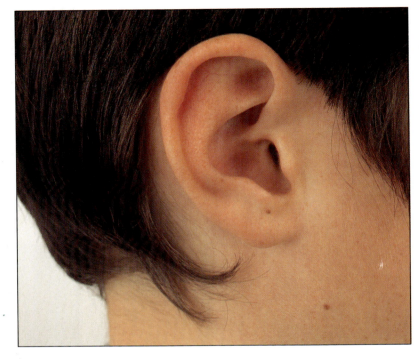

Loud and soft
The messages that are sent to your brain tell it whether the sound is high or low and whether it is loud or soft.

This flute is good at making soft, high sounds.

Sounds

You can hear lots of different types of sound.
You can hear sounds made by people, by animals and by objects.

Close your eyes and listen.
How many different sounds can you hear?

Touching

The sense of touch is to do with your skin.

Skin
Although you can't see them, there are lots of tiny nerves in your skin. These nerves feel things and send messages to your brain about what they feel.

Texture
Some of the nerves in your skin tell your brain about texture, such as whether an object is soft or hard, smooth or rough.

Touch a book. How would you describe its texture?

Danger
Some of the nerves in your skin feel the difference between hot and cold. If something is too hot or too cold, pain messages are sent to your brain, to warn it that your body is in danger.

Pain messages are also sent when you touch sharp things, like the end of a needle, or if you bump into something or fall over.

Tasting and smelling

You use your mouth and nose to taste and smell.

Tongue
Your tongue is covered with little bumps, called taste buds. These tell you whether food is sweet, salty, bitter or sour.

Different parts of your tongue tell you about the different types of taste.

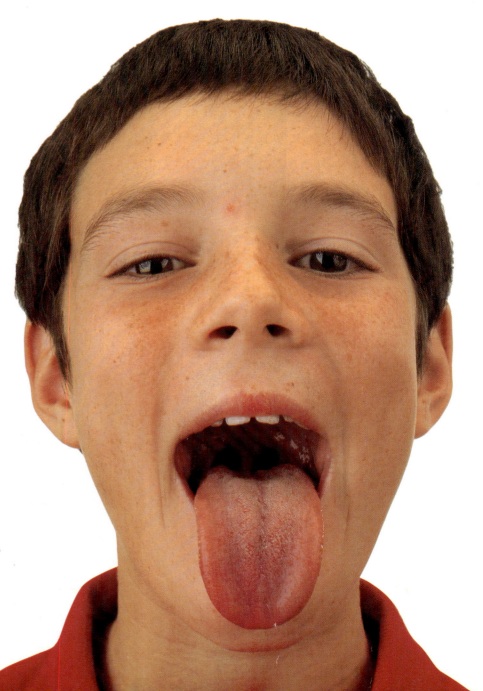

Eating

When you eat a meal, you are smelling your food as well as tasting it.
If you eat something without looking, you can usually guess what it is.
But, if you hold your nose so that you can't smell, it is very difficult to guess.

Memory

Smells are closely linked to memory. They can remind you of people or places.
What is your favourite smell?

Babies

All human beings begin life as babies.

Newborn
This little baby is only a few weeks old.
When you were first born, you weren't able to do very much for yourself.
You could only cry and suck milk and fill your nappy!

Learning

This baby is six months old.
She can sit and crawl and play with toys.
She is learning to feed herself.
Have you got any photographs of yourself as a baby?

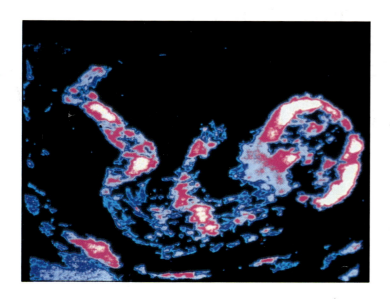

Before birth

Before you were born, you grew inside your mother, in a special place called a uterus.
You spent about nine months in your mother's uterus, growing from a tiny cell into a baby.
This photograph was taken using a special machine that shows a baby inside its mother's uterus.

Growing

As you get older, your body will continue to grow and change.

Now
This boy is seven years old. He is taller and heavier than he was when he was a baby.

How tall are you?
How much do you weigh?

Puberty

At some point, your body will begin to change shape as well as size.
This time of change is called puberty.
It is the time when your body changes from a child's body into a grown-up's body.
These changes happen gradually, over a number of years.

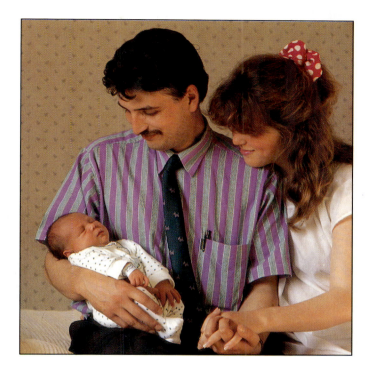

The future

Once all these changes have happened, your body is able to help make babies.

Some time in the future you might decide that you would like to have a baby.

I'm alive

You need food and water to stay alive.

Energy
Food gives your body energy.
Energy keeps your body working.

As you walk and run and play, your body uses energy.

Water
Your body needs water, too. It loses water when you wee. When you are hot, water comes out through your skin as sweat. You replace most of this water with drinks.
Some foods, like strawberries, have lots of water in them, too.

Food
Your body turns food into special chemicals, which it then uses for energy. Some foods, such as bread, potatoes, sugar and butter, are particularly good at giving your body energy.

Keeping healthy

It is not enough just to keep your body going. You have to keep it healthy, too.

Eating

The food you eat isn't just to give you energy. Different foods have different jobs.
Fish and eggs, for instance, are good at helping your body to grow.

Eating the right amount of the right type of food is called having a 'balanced diet'.

Why not find out more about the foods you eat and how they help your body?

Exercise

Exercise is very good for your body.
It makes your heart strong and keeps
your blood healthy.
It is good for your muscles
and your joints.
It is fun, too!

Feeling ill

Sometimes your body becomes unwell.

Germs
Have you ever caught a cold? Illnesses like colds, chicken pox and measles are caused by tiny germs that pass from one person to another. Special injections can stop you getting some of these diseases.

Accidents
Sometimes we injure our bodies by accident.
This girl has broken her arm.
It has been set in plaster to keep the bone in the correct position while it mends.

Medicines

Some illnesses can be cured or helped by medicines. Your doctor might have given you medicine to cure an earache or a sore throat.

Medicines should always be given to you by an adult. The wrong amount of medicine can be very dangerous.

I'm Me!

No two people have bodies that look exactly the same.

Differences
How would you describe what you look like?
Look closely at someone else.
In which ways do you look the same and in what ways do you look different?

Special help

Sometimes, people's bodies need special help.
The girl in the middle of the picture below is not able to walk.
She uses a wheelchair to help her get around.
Some children are not able to hear very well.
They might use hearing aids.

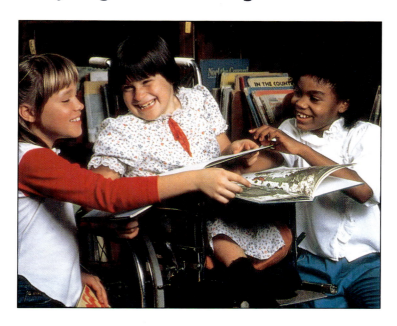

You

But you are more than just your body.
Lots of things go into the making of you.
The things you like doing, the friends you have and the things that make you laugh.
All these and more make the person that is YOU.

Glossary

cells the tiny parts that all animal and plants are made up of
diet the food you usually eat
germs cells that can carry diseases
improve make better
joint where two parts of the body are joined
muscles bundles of thin bands that move parts of the body
nerves thread-like bands that join the brain with all other parts of the body
ray a line or beam of light

Index

accidents 20
arms 3

babies 12–13
body 2–3, 18, 22
brain 6, 9

ears 6–7
eating 11, 18
energy 16–17, 18
exercise 19
eyes 4–5

food 16, 17

glasses 5
growing 14–15, 18

hearing 6–7, 23

injections 20

joints 2, 3

legs 2

medicines 21
memory 11
muscles 19

nerves 6, 8, 9
nose 11

puberty 15

seeing 4–5
skin 8
smelling 10–11
sweat 17

taste buds 10
tasting 10–11
tongue 10
touching 8–9

How to use this book

Each book in this series takes a familiar topic or theme and focuses on one area of the curriculum: science, art and technology, geography or history. The books are intended as starting points, illustrating some of the many different angles from which a topic can be studied. They should act as springboards for further investigation, activity or information seeking.

The following list of books may prove useful.

Further books to read

Series	Title	Author	Publisher
First Starts	All Human Body Titles All Senses Titles	Anita Ganeri Lillian Wright	Watts
Flip Flaps	All Titles	C. Varley	Usborne
Get Set Go!	All Body Titles	Ruth Thomson	Watts
How My Body Works	All Titles	Various	Wayland
Jump! Science	Experiment With Senses	Bryan Murphy	Watts
Look After Yourself	Healthy Food	J. Quinn & A. Qualter	Wayland
Science Activities	Science and Your Body	R. Heddle	Usborne
See For Yourself	Hearing Looking Smell and Taste Touch	Brenda Walpole " " "	A&C Black
Starting Out	My Body My Feet My Hands		Heinemann
Starting Point Science	What's Inside You Where Do Babies Come From? Why Are People Different? Why Do People Eat?	S. Meredith " " K. Needham	Usborne
Your Body	All Titles	Anna Sandeman	Watts